Apostles
Jesus' Special Helpers

EDMON L. ROWELL, JR. • ILLUSTRATED BY JAMES PADGETT

BROADMAN PRESS
Nashville, Tennessee

4242-46
ISBN:0-8054-4246-4

Dewey Decimal Classification; J225.92
Subject heading: APOSTLES

Printed in the United States of America.

Contents

4

Twelve Special Helpers

Jesus walked up to Simon. He looked at
Andrew fishing in the water. "Come, go
with me," he said to them. "I will teach you
to fish for people." Simon and Andrew left

5

their nets, their boat—everything. They followed Jesus.

That is how it began. Jesus called one or two at a time. They went where Jesus went. They listened. They asked questions. Jesus was a great teacher. They wanted to learn. They became Jesus' pupils, learners, or disciples. Many people could be called by these names. But Jesus chose twelve special helpers called apostles.

An apostle is one who is sent out to represent or to do the work of someone in authority. Jesus said he was sent to be God's special representative on earth. Just as God sent him, Jesus said, he sent the apostles.

Peter Spoke for the Twelve

"What do people think of me?" Jesus asked. "Who do they think I am?"

"Well," the disciples answered, "some people say you must be a prophet come back from the dead."

"What about you?" Jesus asked. "Who do *you* think I am?"

"You are the one God promised!" Peter exclaimed. "You are the Son of God!"

Jesus knew who would answer. Peter was the natural leader of the apostles. He was so sure of himself. He often spoke for the rest.

His real name was Simon Bar-Jona, which means Simon the son of John. "Peter" was the name Jesus gave him.

Jesus said to Peter, "Simon, from now on, I'm going to call you Peter." The name Peter means "rock." From that time Simon was usually called Peter. Jesus saw in Peter the leader Peter could become. But he had to learn to trust in Jesus instead of himself before he became a true leader.

The night before Jesus was killed on the cross, Peter promised Jesus he would never let him down. A little later Peter was asleep when Jesus needed him. Still later Peter told some people three times that he did not even know Jesus. The first time Peter failed Jesus because he was tired. The second time Peter was afraid. Peter learned that he could not trust himself. He could not be sure of Peter. But Jesus did not give up on Peter. So Peter learned that he could trust Jesus. Then Peter could really trust himself.

On the day of Pentecost, Peter preached the first sermon about the resurrection of Jesus. Only a few days before Peter had been afraid to admit he even knew Jesus. But on the day of Pentecost Peter proudly claimed to be a follower of Jesus.

When Peter spoke on the day of Pentecost 3,000 more people became disciples of Jesus. Because Peter had learned to trust Jesus many others learned to trust Jesus too.

Thinkback: What was Peter's real name and what does "Peter" mean? How did he live up to his new name?

10

Andrew Brought Others to Jesus

"Simon! Simon!" Breathless from running, Andrew shouted to his brother.

"What is it, Andrew?" Simon asked.

"We have found him! Come and see!"

"Who? What are you talking about?"

"We have found the Messiah, the one the prophets promised would come. John the Baptizer told us. Simon, you just have to come see for yourself!"

Andrew was right, and Simon's whole life was changed because Andrew brought him to Jesus. Another time Andrew and Philip brought some Greeks to meet Jesus. But one of the greatest things happened when Andrew brought a young boy to Jesus. It happened like this . . .

One day there were as many as 5,000 people following Jesus. Many of them had

11

walked all the way around Lake Galilee
just to be near Jesus. Late in the day Jesus
noticed that the people were tired and
hungry.

"What are we going to do?" Jesus asked
his disciples. "Where can we get enough to
feed all these people?"

Andrew stepped up, his arm around a
young boy's shoulder. "Lord," he said,
"this boy has a lunch—two fish and five
small rolls. It is so little, but . . . ."

"Young friend," Jesus asked the boy,
"will you share what you have?"

12

"Yes," the boy said, "but it is so little."

"Don't worry," Jesus said. To Simon Peter he said: "Tell the people to sit down, Peter. We are going to eat!"

The people sat down. When Jesus had finished sharing the fish and rolls, there was more than enough! Jesus used what a young boy shared to help many, many people. It was Andrew who found the boy and brought him to Jesus.

Andrew knew that if he brought others to Jesus, then Jesus would make everything right.

Andrew knew that in Jesus' hands things and people change and become bigger and better. That is why Andrew brought them to Jesus.

Thinkback: Why did Andrew want to bring his brother Simon to meet Jesus? Why was what Andrew did just as important as what his brother Simon Peter did?

James Was Faithful

"Lord, let's burn up this place! They can't treat *us* that way and get away with it!"

James and John, sons of Zebedee, were talking. The people of a small village in Samaria had refused to let Jesus and his disciples spend the night there. So James and John were ready to burn down the town.

"James! John!," Jesus said. "Don't you know that I came to help people, not to hurt them."

Because James and John were so enthusiastic and quick-tempered Jesus nicknamed them "sons of thunder." Like Peter and Andrew they were fishermen in Capernaum.

14

15

Like rough and hardheaded Peter, the "sons of thunder" were changed by Jesus, too. James was probably older than John. James became a leader of the church in Jerusalem. We do not know much more about him. But one thing we do know tells us a lot about the kind of man he became.

About twelve or fifteen years after Jesus was crucified, James was killed by the king. James was killed because he was a Christian and because many people hated the Christians.

A proud, selfish man who wanted to get back at anyone who hurt his feelings—that was the old James. A man who would give up his life before he would be unfaithful to Jesus—that was the new James.

Thinkback: Why were James and John called "sons of thunder"?

Why do you think James gave up his life rather than being unfaithful to Jesus?

John Was a Trusted Friend

"From now on," Jesus said to Mary, "he is your son."

"From now on," he said to John, "she is your mother."

Jesus was on the cross. Standing near the cross, sad and helpless, were Mary and some others. One of those others was John, son of Zebedee.

Jesus trusted John to take care of Mary. From that moment John cared for Mary as

17

if she were his own mother.

Jesus loved all his disciples. He loves us too. But he had a special place in his heart for John. Sometimes John is described as the "disciple whom Jesus loved."

John was James' brother just as Andrew was Peter's brother. Like his brother James, John was quick-tempered and enthusiastic. Like James, John cared deeply about life, about persons.

The Gospel he wrote to tell us about Jesus says: "These are written, that ye might believe that Jesus is the Christ, the Son of God; and that believing ye might have life through his name." One verse from his book—John 3:16—is probably the best known verse in the Bible. It tells us of God's great love for us.

Thinkback: How do we know that Jesus trusted John in a special way?

Why did John write about Jesus?

Do you know that Jesus wants to be your special friend?

19

Philip Was Respected by Others

"Did you see that?!"

"Yes, but I don't believe it. The very idea of chasing those money changers and merchants out of the Temple!"

"Maybe they should be run off, cheating the poor people as they do. But the priests are not going to like it. I wonder who that man is."

"I heard Philip of Bethsaida call him Jesus. He's from Nazareth. Philip said he is the Messiah."

"Let's go meet him and talk with him. Let's ask Philip to introduce us."

It was Passover time in Jerusalem. People had come from everywhere to observe the Jews' most important holiday. Jesus and his apostles were there too.

You may remember how Jesus chased some people out of the Temple. They were money changers who—for a large fee—changed regular money into special Temple money for offerings and sacrifices. The merchants in the Temple who sold animals for sacrifices charged far too much. They cheated poor people. Jesus ran them out of God's house.

A group of curious Greeks saw what happened. They wanted to talk with Jesus, to learn what kind of person he was. They came to Philip and said, "Sir, we want to get to know Jesus." Philip called Andrew and together they introduced the Greeks to Jesus.

Philip was from the town of Bethsaida. Bethsaida was also the hometown of Peter and Andrew.

Philip introduced someone else to Jesus. He brought Nathanael to Jesus. Nathanael found it difficult to believe when Philip said he had found the Messiah. But Nathanael respected Philip and trusted him. So he went with Philip to see for himself. Nathanael—also called Bartholomew—became a disciple of Jesus too.

Philip was not a great preacher like Peter or a great leader like James. But people who knew him respected him and trusted him. So when Philip said something about Jesus, people listened. They trusted Philip and through him they learned to trust Jesus.

Thinkback: Why did the curious Greeks ask Philip to introduce them to Jesus?

What kind of person do you trust and respect?

Should Jesus' helpers always be trustworthy? Why?

22

Bartholomew Looked for God

"Nathanael" means "God's gift" or "God has given." Nathanael is another of Jesus' disciples who has more than one name in the New Testament. He is also called Bartholomew which means "son of Talmai."

As Nathanael Bartholomew grew up, his father taught him from the Scriptures. He also taught him to pray. When he became a man Bartholomew still studied the Scriptures and prayed.

One day a trusted friend from Bethsaida, Philip, came running to

24

25

Bartholomew. "Come see the man I have found. I believe he is the one all the prophets said would come! His name is Jesus. He is from Nazareth."

"Nazareth? Why that's just three miles from my hometown, Cana. I know Nazareth. And I can tell you, no Messiah will ever come from that town!"

Bartholomew went to meet Jesus anyway. When he met him he knew. Jesus was the one he had learned about from the Scriptures. "Teacher," he said to Jesus, "you are the Son of God!" Bartholomew, too, became one of Jesus' disciples. Bartholomew was wrong about Nazareth. God had spoken to Bartholomew through the Scriptures and through prayer. So when he met Jesus he knew that God had sent Jesus too.

Thinkback: Who helped Bartholomew find Jesus? How did Bartholomew know who Jesus was?

Thomas Was Sure About Jesus

"Don't be afraid and don't worry," Jesus
told his disciples one day. "There is a place
for all of you in God's house in heaven.

Soon I am going there to get everything ready for you when you come. You know where I am going. You know the way too."

"What do you mean, Lord?" Thomas blurted out. "We don't know where you are going, so how can we know the way?"

Then Jesus replied, "I am the way, the truth, and the life."

Thomas asked many questions. He wanted to know about things, to understand. So he asked questions.

We do not know much more about Thomas, not even his real name. Thomas is really a nickname. In Aramaic which Jesus spoke it means "twin." He is also called Didymus. Didymus is the Greek word for "twin." So both Thomas and Didymus mean the same—"twin."

When Jesus was crucified, all the disciples were sad and afraid. But they soon learned that Jesus was not really gone. He returned from the grave. He was still very much with them—just as he had promised.

The disciples who first saw the

28

29

resurrected Jesus told Thomas, "We have seen the Lord! He is alive! We've seen him!"

"I don't believe it. "Thomas said. "You're just trying to fool me. I won't believe it until I see him with my own eyes and touch him with my own hands."

Later Thomas did see Jesus. He did not have to touch him to believe. Thomas only wanted to know for himself and understand. When he saw Jesus, he was sure.

Thinkback: Why did Thomas ask questions?

Should we be afraid to ask questions?

Matthew Kept Good Records

"He's eating with those publicans again! How can a man who claims to be sent from God even go near those people?"

The scribes and Pharisees—religious leaders of Jesus' time—were talking about Jesus. Jesus had just called a publican—a tax collector—to be his disciple. Now he was at that tax collector's house eating lunch with him and his friends.

Tax collectors were disliked and mistrusted in Jesus' day. Some tax collectors were dishonest and cheated poor people. Some of them became rich by cheating others. Not all tax collectors were evil men, but because some of them were, they were disliked, even hated. So the religious leaders could not understand why Jesus would even talk with such people. One time Jesus told everyone why he associated with sinners: "I have come," he said, "to find and save those who are lost."

32

We know very little about Matthew. But we do know he kept a careful record of the things Jesus did and said. One day his record became what is called the Gospel of Matthew.

In his Gospel, Matthew included things that are not in the other Gospels. Parts of Jesus' teachings in Matthew 5—7 which we

call the Sermon on the Mount are only in Matthew. "You cannot serve both God and money." "Seek ye first the kingdom of God." These are examples. Matthew had spent much of his life putting money first. Those teachings meant a lot to him. So he remembered them for us.

Thinkback: What was Matthew's occupation when Jesus called him?

Why did many people dislike tax collectors?

Why is it important that Matthew knew how to keep good records?

James, Son of Alphaeus, Was Somebody

The last part of Genesis 1:16 says "he made the stars also." Everyone notices the sun and the moon. But some people never notice the stars. People are like that too.

There are a few people who shine like the sun and the moon. Many people, however, are like the stars. They are "alsos."

James the son of Alphaeus was an "also." The New Testament tells us almost nothing about him except his name. We do not know anything he did. We do not know anything he said. Nothing. Just his name.

Sometimes this apostle known as James was called James the Less or James the Younger. This would help people from getting him mixed up with James the son of Zebedee.

As far as the world is concerned, James the son of Alphaeus was almost nobody. Yet Jesus called him to be his special helper. Jesus saw something in James the Less. Jesus wanted him as a special helper.

Thinkback: Why is James the Less an important apostle? What was another name he was called?

Thaddaeus Wanted Jesus to Take Over

"In a little while," Jesus told his disciples at the Last Supper, "I must go away. But I will come back to you soon. You will see me, but the world will not."

"What is happening, Lord?" exclaimed

one of the twelve. "What do you mean we will see you but the world will not?"

Thaddaeus was the one who asked the questions. To understand his question we must understand the situation.

During Jesus' time the whole Jewish nation was under the rule of the Romans. Their whole life was run by the Roman government. They had to pay high taxes to support the Roman government too.

There were some Jews who wanted to revolt against Rome and set up their own government again. Some of Jesus' disciples expected Jesus to become king and take over the world. They were surprised and disappointed when Jesus said that in a little while the world would not see him anymore.

Jesus could have taken charge and ruled the world by force. But that is not God's way. God does not want us to obey him and be good because he forces us. He wants us to obey him because we love him and want to be good. Thaddaeus had to learn that.

Thaddaeus has been called "Trinomius"

which means "the one with three names."
Thaddaeus' real name was probably
Judas, the son of James. We do not know
which James. Sometimes he was called
"Judas, not Iscariot." But Judas became an
unpopular name so he was nicknamed
Thaddaeus which means "bold" or
"lively." He was also called Lebbaeus which
means "enthusiastic" or "courageous."

We know very little more about Judas,
nicknamed Thaddaeus and Lebbaeus. But
we do know that he kept on being a
disciple. He learned that God does not
always do things the way we think he ought
to. Instead, God does things his way.
Thaddaeus had to learn that. All of Jesus'
helpers have to learn that.

Thinkback: What did Thaddaeus want
Jesus to do instead of dying on the
cross?

Simon Zelotes Turned from Hate to Love

The New Testament tells us nothing about Simon Zelotes except his name. But we can discover a lot about him just by his name.

Zelotes was not his real name, but a word that described him. It meant that Simon belonged to a group called the Zealots.

41

At first the Zealots were a group of Jews who wanted to keep the Jewish law pure and unbroken. They punished anyone they caught breaking the law. When Jesus drove the merchants and money changers from the Temple, his disciples thought he might be a Zealot. But he was not.

Later the Zealots became more interested in freedom from Roman rule. Some Zealots would do anything to make the Romans leave Israel. Some Zealots even killed with a dagger the Romans the Zealots thought broke the Jewish law.

When Simon became Jesus' disciple he still wanted people to be law-abiding and to honor God. But instead of trying to force people to obey the law and hurting or even killing those who did not, he learned to love, to forgive and to help just like Jesus.

Thinkback: Who were the Zealots?
How did Simon Zelotes change when he became Jesus' disciple?

42

Judas Was Sorry Too Late

"Take back your dirty money! I don't want it! Turn Jesus loose! He is innocent!"

Judas was in the Temple yelling at the religious leaders to take back their bribe money. Just a few hours before they had given Judas thirty pieces of silver. In return Judas had told them where they could find Jesus.

The religious leaders arrested Jesus.

Now he was on trial. Very soon he would be condemned to death on a cross. Judas wanted to undo what he had done. But it was too late.

The ones who wanted Jesus dead would not release Jesus. They would not take back the money either. So Judas threw the money on the Temple floor, went away, and hanged himself.

Judas began as one of Jesus' special helpers too. Jesus and the others trusted him so much that they made him treasurer

45

for the group. He was the one who took care of all their money and paid their way as they traveled around preaching and teaching.

Judas learned too late that God's way is sacrificing love, not selfish force. Judas was sorry, but the harm was already done and could not be undone.

Like all the rest—and like you and me, too—Judas was a mixture of good and evil. In Judas, however, the evil won over the good. Judas could not live with what he had done. He was sorry, but it was too late.

Thinkback: What special job did Judas have as one of Jesus' special helpers.

Why do you think Judas wanted to give the money back to the priests?

HARAN

NINEVEH

SUSA

BABYLON

SHUNEM

DAMASCUS

MT. TABOR

MT. CARMEL

DOTHAN

BETHEL

ANATHOTH

JERUSALEM

TIMNAH

BETHLEHEM

GAZA

JERICHO

JOPPA

GILGAL

MT. NEBO

GERAR

MORESHETH

HEBRON

TEKOA

EGYPT

SOME OLD TESTAMENT
PLACES

Reflections

- Each apostle was different. Each one could do something special. Peter could speak well in public. Andrew knew how to bring others to Jesus. Matthew knew how to keep good records. You are special too. There is something special that you can do. Jesus wants all of us to be his helpers.

- Following Jesus made a difference in the apostles. They were all changed. What the apostles once had done for themselves they began doing for Jesus. That made a real difference. When you and I begin following Jesus it makes a difference in us too.

- The apostles can teach us that Jesus can take whatever we have and make it better. We should never refuse to be Jesus' helper simply because we think we have only a little to offer. Remember Andrew and the little boy with a small lunch? Whatever we give to Jesus for his use will be multiplied in his hands.